WORDSWORTH

Compiled and Illustrated
by
Patricia Machin

Salem House Publishers
Topsfield, Massachusetts

First published in the United States by Salem House
Publishers, 1987
462 Boston Street, Topsfield, MA 01983

Library of Congress Cataloging in-Publication Data
Wordsworth, William, 1770-1850.
  Wordsworth.
  I. Machin, Patricia, 1920-   II. Title.
  PR5853.M33   1987   821'.7   87-9480

  ISBN 0-88162-298-2

First published in Great Britain 1985 by
Webb & Bower (Publishers) Limited
9 Colleton Crescent, Exeter, Devon EX2 4BY

Typeset in Great Britain by P&M Typesetting Limited,
Exeter, Devon

Printed and bound in Hong Kong by Mandarin Offset
International Limited

Contents

Introduction

William Wordsworth was born at Cockermouth in 1770; he had four brothers and one sister, Dorothy. By the time he was thirteen both his parents had died, and due to the debt the Earl of Lonsdale had incurred with their father (who had been his lawyer and agent) the orphaned children were left in humble circumstances. Nevertheless, it was made possible for the boys to be sent to school at Hawkshead where they boarded with a 'Dame' during term-time, and where Wordsworth found much happiness and freedom in the beautiful and varied lakeland country surrounding the school.

This intense enjoyment of nature was sustained throughout the poet's life and formed the essence of his early masterpieces, so entirely new in feeling that they were received with derision until their freshness of style and originality were understood.

Wordsworth was one of the young men of that period whose imagination was fired by the aspirations of the French towards freedom, and after taking a degree at Cambridge in 1791 he spent a year in France. Later, when he saw that with the French Revolution came cruelty and violence and not the long desired ideal state, he became disillusioned.

There followed some years of hardship and uncertainty. Then he was left a small legacy enabling him to settle with his sister in Somerset and later in the Lake District where he remained for the rest of his life, marrying his life-long friend and cousin, Mary Hutchinson, in 1802.

In 1813 he became Distributor of Stamps in Westmorland, ensuring him a steady income for his family, and in 1843 he was appointed Poet Laureate on the death of Robert Southey, another Lakeland poet.

Much has been written over the years about Wordsworth and his poetry. The poet S T Coleridge with whom he had a long and mutually inspiring friendship wrote of him: 'He was the nearest of all modern writers to Shakespeare and Milton yet in a kind perfectly unborrowed and his own.'

R W Church, in 1888, listed his attributes: 'His austere purity and perfection of language, the wideness of his range, the freshness of his thought, the unfailing certainty of his eye; his unswerving truth, and, above all, his magnificent gift of imagination.'

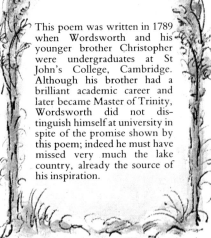

This poem was written in 1789 when Wordsworth and his younger brother Christopher were undergraduates at St John's College, Cambridge. Although his brother had a brilliant academic career and later became Master of Trinity, Wordsworth did not distinguish himself at university in spite of the promise shown by this poem; indeed he must have missed very much the lake country, already the source of his inspiration.

Lines

WRITTEN WHILE SAILING IN A BOAT AT EVENING

How richly glows the water's breast
Before us, tinged with evening hues,
While, facing thus the crimson west,
The boat her silent course pursues!
And see how dark the backward stream!
A little moment past so smiling!
And still, perhaps, with faithless gleam,
Some other loiterers beguiling.

Such views the youthful Bard allure;
But, heedless of the following gloom,
He deems their colours shall endure
Till peace go with him to the tomb.
—And let him nurse his fond deceit,
And what if he must die in sorrow!
Who would not cherish dreams so sweet,
Though grief and pain may come to-morrow?

'Actually composed while I was sitting by the side of a brook that runs down from the comb, in which stands the village of Alford, through the grounds of Alfoxden. It was a chosen resort of mine,' wrote Wordsworth of this beautiful early lyric, written in 1798. His early work, published with some poems of Coleridge and marking a revival of English poetry, was at first unfavourably received.

Lines Written in Early Spring

I HEARD a thousand blended notes,
While in a grove I sate reclined,
In that sweet mood when pleasant thoughts
Bring sad thoughts to the mind.

To her fair works did Nature link
The human soul that through me ran;
And much it grieved my heart to think
What man has made of man.

Through primrose tufts, in that green bower,
The periwinkle trailed its wreaths;
And 'tis my faith that every flower
Enjoys the air it breathes.

The birds around me hopped and played,
Their thoughts I cannot measure:—
But the least motion which they made,
It seemed a thrill of pleasure.

The budding twigs spread out their fan,
To catch the breezy air;
And I must think, do all I can,
That there was pleasure there.

If this belief from heaven be sent,
If such be Nature's holy plan,
Have I not reason to lament
What man has made of man?

These two poems are a reminder that death in childhood was no rare event in Wordsworth's time and the suffering and grief that it entailed was often movingly described by the poet and his contemporaries. 'There was a Boy' was one of many poems he completed at Goslar, Northern Germany, where the exceptionally severe winter of 1798-9 caused the poet and his sister Dorothy to prolong their stay. Wordsworth wrote an account of the town and their lodgings, also a poem 'Written on one of the Coldest Days of the Century'.

'We are Seven' was written in 1798 at Alfoxden.

There was a Boy

THERE was a Boy; ye knew him well, ye cliffs
And islands of Winander!–many a time,
At evening, when the earliest stars began
To move along the edges of the hills,
Rising or setting, would he stand alone,
Beneath the trees, or by the glimmering lake;
And there, with fingers interwoven, both hands
Pressed closely palm to palm and to his mouth
Uplifted, he, as through an instrument,
Blew mimic hootings to the silent owls,
That they might answer him.–And they would shout
Across the watery vale, and shout again,
Responsive to his call,–with quivering peals,
And long halloos, and screams, and echoes loud
Redoubled and redoubled; concourse wild
Of jocund din! And, when there came a pause
Of silence such as baffled his best skill:
Then, sometimes, in that silence, while he hung,
Listening, a gentle shock of mild surprise
Has carried far into his heart the voice
Of mountain-torrents; or the visible scene
Would enter unawares into his mind
With all its solemn imagery, its rocks,
Its woods, and that uncertain heaven received
Into the bosom of the steady lake.
    This boy was taken from his mates, and died
In childhood, ere he was full twelve years old.
Pre-eminent in beauty is the vale
Where he was born and bred: the churchyard hangs
Upon a slope above the village-school;
And, through that churchyard when my way has led
On summer-evenings, I believe, that there
A long half-hour together I have stood
Mute–looking at the grave in which he lies!

We are Seven

—A SIMPLE Child,
That lightly draws its breath,
And feels its life in every limb,
What should it know of death?

I met a little cottage Girl;
She was eight years old, she said;
Her hair was thick with many a
        curl
That clustered round her head.

She had a rustic, woodland air,
And she was wildly clad:
Her eyes were fair, and very fair;
—Her beauty made me glad.

'Sisters and brothers, little maid,
How many may you be?'
'How many? Seven in all,' she
        said,
And wondering looked at me.

'And where are they? I pray you tell.'
She answered, 'Seven are we;
And two of us at Conway dwell,
And two are gone to sea.

'Two of us in the church-yard lie,
My sister and my brother;
And, in the church-yard cottage, I
Dwell near them with my mother.'

'You say that two at Conway dwell,
And two are gone to sea,
Yet ye are seven! I pray you tell,
Sweet Maid, how this may be.'

Then did the little Maid reply,
'Seven boys and girls are we;
Two of us in the church-yard lie,
Beneath the church-yard tree.'

'You run about, my little Maid,
Your limbs they are alive;
If two are in the church-yard laid,
Then ye are only five.'

'So in the church-yard she was laid;
And, when the grass was dry,
Together round her grave we played,
My brother John and I.

'And when the ground was white
                         with snow,
And I could run and slide,
My brother John was forced to go,
And he lies by her side.'

'How many are you, then,' said I,
'If they two are in heaven?'
Quick was the little Maid's reply,
'O Master! we are seven.'

'But they are dead; those two are dead!
Their spirits are in heaven!'
'Twas throwing words away; for still
The little Maid would have her will,
And said, 'Nay, we are seven!'

'Their graves are green, they may be seen.'
The little Maid replied,
'Twelve steps or more from my mother's door,
And they are side by side.

'My stockings there I often knit,
My kerchief there I hem;
And there upon the ground I sit,
And sing a song to them.

'And often after sun-set, Sir,
When it is light and fair,
I take my little porringer,
And eat my supper there.

'The first that died was sister Jane;
In bed she moaning lay,
Till God released her of her pain;
And then she went away.

This short masterpiece was
written in 1802, the same
year as the first part of
Wordsworth's famous 'Ode:
Intimations of Immortality'.
It was also at this time that he
and his sister Dorothy began
to drift apart from the poet
Coleridge, whose close
association with Wordsworth
had been so productive for
both poets and whose
Biographia Literaria, published
in 1817, contains a most
stimulating document on
Wordsworth.

My heart leaps up when I behold
   A rainbow in the sky:
So was it when my life began;
So is it now I am a man;
So be it when I shall grow old,
   Or let me die!
The Child is father of the Man;
And I could wish my days to be
Bound each to each by natural piety.

Wordsworth's sister Dorothy not only kept house for him before he married but also inspired and encouraged him unfailingly. Her unusual understanding and close observation of nature is evident from her journals and the details she recorded must have been immensely useful to the poet. She would no doubt have been greatly surprised had she known that her journals themselves would one day rank as a classic work.

This poem was composed in front of Alfoxden House; the child was the son of Wordsworth's friend, Basil Montagu.

To my Sister

It is the first mild day of March:
Each minute sweeter than before,
The redbreast sings from the tall larch
That stands beside our door.

There is a blessing in the air,
Which seems a sense of joy to yield
To the bare trees, and mountains bare,
And grass in the green field.

My sister! ('tis a wish of mine)
Now that our morning meal is done,
Make haste, your morning task resign;
Come forth and feel the sun.

Edward will come with you;–and, pray,
Put on with speed your woodland dress;
And bring no book; for this one day
We'll give to idleness.

No joyless forms shall regulate
Our living calendar:
We from to-day, my Friend, will date
The opening of the year.

Love, now a universal birth,
From heart to heart is stealing,
From earth to man, from man to earth:
–It is the hour of feeling.

One moment now may give us more
Than years of toiling reason:
Our minds shall drink at every pore
The spirit of the season.

Some silent laws our hearts will make,
Which they shall long obey:
We for the year to come may take
Our temper from to-day.

And from the blessed power that rolls
About, below, above,
We'll frame the measure of our souls:
They shall be tuned to love.

Then come, my Sister! come, I pray,
With speed put on your woodland dress;
And bring no book: for this one day
We'll give to idleness.

'To a Butterfly', written in the orchard at Dove Cottage in 1802, is evidence of Wordsworth's memory for all the details of his childhood pleasures.

'Anecdote for Fathers' was written at Alfoxden in 1798; it describes the reaction of a small child when pressed too hard for a logical reason for a preference which is beyond his comprehension – perhaps the relentless adult deserved the nonsensical answer he received!

To a Butterfly

STAY near me–do not take thy flight!
A little longer stay in sight!
Much converse do I find in thee,
Historian of my infancy!
Float near me; do not yet depart!
Dead times revive in thee:
Thou bring'st, gay creature as thou art!
A solemn image to my heart,
My father's family!

Oh! pleasant, pleasant were the days,
The time, when, in our childish plays,
My sister Emmeline and I
Together chased the butterfly!
A very hunter did I rush
Upon the prey:–with leaps and springs
I followed on from brake to bush;
But she, God love her, feared to brush
The dust from off its wings.

Anecdote for Fathers

I HAVE a boy of five years old;
His face is fair and fresh to see;
His limbs are cast in beauty's mould,
And dearly he loves me.

One morn we strolled on our dry walk,
Our quiet home all full in view,
And held such intermitted talk
As we are wont to do.

My thoughts on former pleasures ran;
I thought of Kilve's delightful shore,
Our pleasant home when spring began,
A long, long year before.

A day it was when I could bear
Some fond regrets to entertain;
With so much happiness to spare,
I could not feel a pain.

The green earth echoed to the feet
Of lambs that bounded through the glade,
From shade to sunshine, and as fleet
From sunshine back to shade.

Birds warbled round me–and each trace
Of inward sadness had its charm;
Kilve, thought I, was a favoured place,
And so is Liswyn farm.

My boy beside me tripped, so slim
And graceful in his rustic dress!
And, as we talked, I questioned him,
In very idleness.

'Now tell me, had you rather be,'
I said, and took him by the arm,
'On Kilve's smooth shore,
                    by the green sea,
Or here at Liswyn farm?'

In careless mood he looked at me,
While still I held him by the arm,
And said, 'At Kilve I'd rather be
Than here at Liswyn farm.'

'Now, little Edward, say why so:
My little Edward, tell me why.'–
'I cannot tell, I do not know.'–
'Why, this is strange,' said I;

'For here are woods, hills smooth and warm:
There surely must some reason be
Why you would change sweet Liswyn farm
For Kilve by the green sea.'

At this my boy hung down his head,
He blushed with shame, nor made reply;
And three times to the child I said,
'Why, Edward, tell me why?'

His head he raised–there was in sight,
It caught his eye, he saw it plain–
Upon the house-top, glittering bright,
A broad and gilded vane.

Then did the boy his tongue unlock,
And eased his mind with this reply:
'At Kilve there was no weather-cock;
And that's the reason why.'

O dearest, dearest boy! my heart
For better lore would seldom yearn,
Could I but teach the hundredth part
Of what from thee I learn.

'Written at Town-end, Grasmere. The daffodils grew, and still grow on the margin of Ullswater' wrote Wordsworth of this poem, possibly the best loved of his lyrics, written in 1804. Dorothy wrote in her journal: 'I never saw daffodils so beautiful. They grew among the mossy stones about and above them; some rested their heads upon the stones, as on a pillow, for weariness; and the rest tossed and reeled and danced, and seemed as if they verily laughed with the wind, that blew upon them over the lake.'

I WANDERED lonely as a cloud
That floats on high o'er vales and hills,
When all at once I saw a crowd,
A host, of golden daffodils;
Beside the lake, beneath the trees,
Fluttering and dancing in the breeze.

Continuous as the stars that shine
And twinkle on the milky way,
They stretched in never-ending line
Along the margin of a bay:
Ten thousand saw I at a glance,
Tossing their heads in sprightly dance.

The waves beside them danced; but they
Out-did the sparkling waves in glee:
A poet could not but be gay,
In such a jocund company:
I gazed–and gazed–but little thought
What wealth the show to me had brought:

For oft, when on my couch I lie
In vacant or in pensive mood,
They flash upon that inward eye
Which is the bliss of solitude;
And then my heart with pleasure fills,
And dances with the daffodils.

'Composed while we were labouring together in his pleasure-ground' wrote Wordsworth of his poem 'To the Spade of a Friend'. Thomas Wilkinson, a Quaker, was his friend and the poet, always keenly observant, must have understood the loving care he took of his tools. Four verses of the poem are illustrated here.

'Repentance' was written in 1804. The ideas for Wordsworth's ballads were often obtained in conversation with local people, in this case with his neighbour Margaret Ashburner.

To the Spade of a Friend

COMPOSED WHILE WE WERE LABOURING TOGETHER IN HIS PLEASURE-GROUND

SPADE! with which Wilkinson hath tilled his lands,
And shaped these pleasant walks by Emont's side,
Thou art a tool of honour in my hands;
I press thee, through the yielding soil, with pride.

Rare master has it been thy lot to know;
Long hast Thou served a man to reason true;
Whose life combines the best of high and low,
The labouring many and the resting few;

Here often hast Thou heard the Poet sing
In concord with his river murmuring by;
Or in some silent field, while timid spring
Is yet uncheered by other minstrelsy.

Who shall inherit Thee when death has laid
Low in the darksome cell thine own dear lord?
That man will have a trophy, humble Spade!
A trophy nobler than a conqueror's sword.

Repentance

A Pastoral Ballad

The fields which with covetous spirit we sold,
Those beautiful fields, the delight of the day,
Would have brought us more good than a burthen of gold,
Could we but have been as contented as they.

When the troublesome Tempter beset us, said I,
"Let him come, with his purse proudly grasped in his hand
But, Allan, be true to me, Allan,—we'll die
Before he shall go with an inch of the land!"

There dwelt we, as happy as birds in their bowers;
Unfettered as bees that in gardens abide;
We could do what we liked with the land, it was ours;
And for us the brook murmured that ran by its side.

But now we are strangers, go early or late;
And often, like one overburthened with sin,
With my hand on the latch of the half-opened gate,
I look at the fields, but I cannot go in!

When I walk by the hedge on a bright summer's day,
Or sit in the shade of my grandfather's tree,
A stern face it puts on, as if ready to say,
"What ails you, that you must come creeping to me!"

With our pastures about us, we could not be sad;
Our comfort was near if we ever were crost;
But the comfort, the blessings, and wealth that we had,
We slighted them all,–and our birth-right was lost.

Oh, ill-judging sire of an innocent son
Who must now be a wanderer! but peace to that strain!
Think of evening's repose when our labour was done,
The sabbath's return; and its leisure's soft chain!

And in sickness, if night had been sparing of sleep,
How cheerful, at sunrise, the hill where I stood,
Looking down on the kine, and our treasure of sheep
That besprinkled the field; 'twas like youth in my blood!

Now I cleave to the house, and am dull as a snail;
And, oftentimes, hear the church-bell with a sigh,
That follows the thought–We've no land in the vale,
Save six feet of earth where our forefathers lie!

Many of Wordsworth's poems, like this one, recall the intense happiness of his boyhood, much of which was spent at boarding-school at Hawkshead, the centre of one of the most beautiful areas in the Lake District. He was particularly fortunate in the freedom he was given to roam the countryside for miles around and to occupy himself with the rural pastimes he wrote of later – such as nutting, fishing, bird-nesting, skating – rather than the conventional sports associated with boarding school.

To the Cuckoo

O BLITHE New-comer! I
      have heard,
I hear thee and rejoice.
O Cuckoo! shall I call thee Bird,
Or but a wandering Voice?

While I am lying on the grass
Thy twofold shout I hear,
From hill to hill it seems to pass
At once far off, and near.

Though babbling only to the
      Vale,
Of sunshine and of flowers,
Thou bringest unto me a tale
Of visionary hours.

Thrice welcome, darling of the
      Spring!
Even yet thou art to me
No bird, but an invisible thing,
A voice, a mystery;

The same whom in my
      schoolboy days
I listened to; that Cry
Which made me look a
      thousand ways
In bush, and tree, and sky.

To seek thee did I often rove
Through woods and on the green;
And thou wert still a hope, a love;
Still longed for, never seen.

And I can listen to thee yet;
Can lie upon the plain
And listen, till I do beget
That golden time again.

O Blessèd Bird! the earth we pace
Again appears to be
An unsubstantial, faery place;
That is fit home for Thee!

Written by Wordsworth at the height of his powers, this poem is one of the masterpieces of English poetry. Its astonishing visionary beauty and radiance of light, unsurpassed in any of his later works, classes the poet with his great contemporary, J M W Turner, the English landscape painter of light. The first part of the poem, illustrated here, was begun in March 1802; the poet did not complete it for more than a year.

Ode: Intimations of Immortality from Recollections of Early Childhood

THERE was a time when meadow, grove, and stream,
The earth, and every common sight,
    To me did seem
    Apparelled in celestial light,
The glory and the freshness of a dream.
It is not now as it hath been of yore;–
    Turn wheresoe'er I may,
    By night or day,
The things which I have seen I now can see no more.

    The Rainbow comes and goes,
    And lovely is the Rose,
    The Moon doth with delight
Look round her when the heavens are bare;
    Waters on a starry night
    Are beautiful and fair;
    The sunshine is a glorious birth;
    But yet I know, where'er I go,
That there hath past away a glory from the earth.

Now, while the birds thus sing a joyous song,
    And while the young lambs bound
        As to the tabor's sound,
To me alone there came a thought of grief:
A timely utterance gave that thought relief,
        And I again am strong:
The cataracts blow their trumpets from the steep;
No more shall grief of mine the season wrong;
I hear the Echoes through the mountains throng,
The Winds come to me from the fields of sleep,
        And all the earth is gay;
            Land and sea
        Give themselves up to jollity,
            And with the heart of May
        Doth every Beast keep holiday;—
            Thou Child of Joy,
Shout round me, let me hear thy shouts, thou happy
        Shepherd-boy!

Ye blessèd Creatures, I have heard the call
    Ye to each other make; I see
The heavens laugh with you in your jubilee;
    My heart is at your festival,
        My head hath its coronal,
The fulness of your bliss, I feel–I feel it all.
        Oh evil day! if I were sullen
        While Earth herself is adorning,
            This sweet May-morning,
        And the Children are culling
            On every side,
        In a thousand valleys far and wide,
        Fresh flowers; while the sun shines warm,
And the Babe leaps up on his Mother's arm:–
        I hear, I hear, with joy I hear!
        –But there's a Tree, of many, one,
A single Field which I have looked upon,
Both of them speak of something that is gone:
        The Pansy at my feet
        Doth the same tale repeat:
Whither is fled the visionary gleam?
Where is it now, the glory and the dream?

'The Green Linnet' (of which four verses are illustrated) was written in the orchard at Dove Cottage where so many of Wordsworth's finest poems were composed. When the poet and his family moved to a larger house the writer Thomas de Quincey, who had revered Wordsworth all his life, became the tenant. The Wordsworths did not sustain their friendship with de Quincey after he published *Recollections of the Lakes and the Lake Poets*; they considered he had betrayed their trust in him by making public his observations on their characters and life-style.

The Green Linnet

BENEATH these fruit-tree boughs that shed
Their snow-white blossoms on my head,
With brightest sunshine round me spread
  Of spring's unclouded weather,
In this sequestered nook how sweet
To sit upon my orchard-seat!
And birds and flowers once more to greet,
  My last year's friends together.

One have I marked, the happiest guest
In all this covert of the blest:
Hail to Thee, far above the rest
  In joy of voice and pinion!
Thou, Linnet! in thy green array,
Presiding Spirit here to-day,
Dost lead the revels of the May;
  And this is thy dominion.

While birds, and butterflies, and flowers,
Make all one band of paramours,
Thou, ranging up and down the bowers,
  Art sole in thy employment:
A Life, a Presence like the Air,
Scattering thy gladness without care,
Too blest with any one to pair;
  Thyself thy own enjoyment.

In August 1803 Wordsworth,
Dorothy and Coleridge began
a tour of Scotland; this is
one of the poems that re-
sulted from their travels during
which they visited lochs and
castles and were told the local
legends. Wordsworth wrote:
'Poor Coleridge was at that
time in bad spirits and some-
what too much in love with his
own dejection' – he left the poet
and his sister when they had
only reached Loch Lomond.

The Solitary Reaper

BEHOLD her, single in the field,
Yon solitary Highland Lass!
Reaping and singing by herself;
Stop here, or gently pass!
Alone she cuts and binds the grain,
And sings a melancholy strain;
O listen! for the Vale profound
Is overflowing with the sound.

No Nightingale did ever chaunt
More welcome notes to weary bands
Of travellers in some shady haunt,
Among Arabian sands:
A voice so thrilling ne'er was heard
In spring-time from the cuckoo-bird,
Breaking the silence of the seas
Among the farthest Hebrides.

Will no one tell me what she sings?—
Perhaps the plaintive numbers flow
For old, unhappy, far-off things,
And battles long ago:
Or is it some more humble lay,
Familiar matter of to-day?
Some natural sorrow, loss, or pain,
That has been, and may be again?

Whate'er the theme, the Maiden sang
As if her song could have no ending;
I saw her singing at her work,
And o'er the sickle bending:—
I listened, motionless and still;
And, as I mounted up the hill,
The music in my heart I bore,
Long after it was heard no more.

This poem, written
to his wife, Mary,
is considered one of
Wordsworth's outstanding
lyrics. The poet wrote of it:
'The germ of this poem was
four lines composed as a part of
the verses on "The Highland
girl." Though beginning in this
way, it was written from my
heart, as is sufficiently obvious.'
De Quincey in his *Lakeland
Poets* describes Mary as
possessing 'a sunny
benignity – a
radiant
gracefulness – such as in this
world I never saw equalled
or approached.'

SHE was a Phantom of delight
When first she gleamed upon my sight;
A lovely Apparition, sent
To be a moment's ornament;
Her eyes as stars of Twilight fair;
Like Twilight's, too, her dusky hair;
But all things else about her drawn
From May-time and the cheerful Dawn;
A dancing Shape, an Image gay,
To haunt, to startle, and way-lay.

I saw her upon nearer view,
A Spirit, yet a Woman too!
Her household motions light and free,
And steps of virgin-liberty;
A countenance in which did meet
Sweet records, promises as sweet;
A Creature not too bright or good
For human nature's daily food;
For transient sorrows, simple wiles,
Praise, blame, love, kisses, tears, and smiles.

And now I see with eye serene
The very pulse of the machine;
A Being breathing thoughtful breath,
A Traveller between life and death;
The reason firm, the temperate will,
Endurance, foresight, strength, and skill;
A perfect Woman, nobly planned,
To warn, to comfort, and command;
And yet a Spirit still, and bright
With something of angelic light.

'The Sparrow's Nest', written in the orchard at Grasmere, where so many of Wordsworth's best poems were composed, again recalls his childhood with special reference to his sister Dorothy who also provided the idea for 'Beggars'.

'Written at Townend, Grasmere,' wrote Wordsworth, 'Met and described to me by my sister, near the quarry at the head of Rydal lake, a place still used by vagrants travelling with their families.'

The Sparrow's Nest

Behold, within the leafy shade,
Those bright blue eggs together laid!
On me the chance-discovered sight
Gleamed like a vision of delight.
I started – seeming to espy
The home and sheltered bed,
The Sparrow's dwelling, which, hard by
My Father's house, in wet or dry
My sister Emmeline and I
   Together visited.

She looked at it and seemed to fear it;
Dreading, tho' wishing, to be near it:
Such heart was in her, being then
A little Prattler among men.
The Blessing of my later years
Was with me when a boy;
She gave me eyes, she gave me ears;
And humble cares, and delicate fears;
A heart, the fountain of sweet tears;
   And love, and thought, and joy.

Beggars

She had a tall man's height or more;
Her face from summer's noontide heat
No bonnet shaded, but she wore
A mantle, to her feet
Descending with a graceful flow,
And on her head a cap as white as new-fallen snow.

Her skin was of Egyptian brown:
Haughty, as if her eye had seen
Its own light to a distant thrown,
She towered, fit person for a Queen
To lead those ancient Amazonian files;
Or ruling Bandit's wife among the Grecian isles.

Advancing, forth she stretched her hand
And begged an alms with doleful plea
That ceased not; on our English land
Such woes, I knew, could never be;
And yet a boon I gave her, for the creature
Was beautiful to see – a weed of glorious feature.

I left her, and pursued my way;
And soon before me did espy
A pair of little Boys at play,
Chasing a crimson butterfly;
The taller followed with his hat in hand,
Wreathed round with yellow flowers the gayest of the land.

The other wore a rimles crown
With leaves of laurel stuck about;
And while both followed up and down,
Each whooping with a merry shout,
In their fraternal features I could trace
Unquestionable lines of that wild Suppliant's face.

Yet *they*, so blithe of heart, seemed fit
For the finest tasks of earth or air:
Wings let them have, and they might flit
Precursors to Aurora's car,
Scattering fresh flowers; though happier far, I ween,
To hunt their fluttering game o'er rock and level green.

They dart across my path – but lo,
Each ready with a plaintive whine!
Said I, 'not half an hur ago
Your Mother has had alms of mine.'
'That cannot be,' one answered – 'she is dead:' –
I looked reproof – they saw – but neither hung his head.

'She has been dead, Sir, many a day.' –
'Hush boys! you're telling me a lie;
It was your Mother, as I say!'
And, in the twinkling of an eye,
'Come! come!' cried one, and without more ado
Off to some other play the joyous Vagrants flew!

The Prelude, from which two episodes are illustrated here, is said to be Wordsworth's greatest work. It vividly recalls incidents in the poet's early life and is interwoven with recollections of a deeper kind concerning the mystery of immortality and creative inspiration. He regarded this poem as preparation for a great philosophical work to be called *The Recluse* which never materialized. He would not allow this poem to be published until after his death, when his wife chose the title.

Lines from the Prelude

And in the frosty season, when the sun
Was set, and visible for many a mile
The cottage windows blazed through twilight gloom,
I heeded not their summons: happy time
It was indeed for all of us–for me
It was a time of rapture! Clear and loud
The village clock tolled six,–I wheeled about,
Proud and exulting like an untired horse
That cares not for his home. All shod with steel,
We hissed along the polished ice in games
Confederate, imitative of the chase
And woodland pleasures,–the resounding horn,
The pack loud chiming, and the hunted hare.
So through the darkness and the cold we flew,
And not a voice was idle; with the din
Smitten, the precipices rang aloud;
The leafless trees and every icy crag
Tinkled like iron; while far distant hills
Into the tumult sent an alien sound
Of melancholy not unnoticed, while the stars
Eastward were sparkling clear, and in the west
The orange sky of evening died away.

But now to school
From the half-yearly holidays returned,
We came with weightier purses, that sufficed
To furnish treats more costly than the Dame
Of the old grey stone, from her scant board, supplied.
Hence rustic dinners on the cool green ground,
Or in the woods, or by a river side
Or shady fountains, while among the leaves
Soft airs were stirring, and the mid-day sun
Unfelt shone brightly round us in our joy.
Nor is my aim neglected if I tell
How sometimes, in the length of those half-years,
We from our funds drew largely;–proud to curb,
And eager to spur on, the galloping steed;
And with the courteous inn-keeper, whose stud
Supplied our want, we haply might employ
Sly subterfuge, if the adventure's bound
Were distant: some famed temple where of yore
The Druids worshipped, or the antique walls
Of that large abbey, where within the Vale
Of Nightshade, to St. Mary's honour built,
Stands yet a mouldering pile with fractured arch,
Belfry, and images, and living trees,
A holy scene! Along the smooth green turf
Our horses grazed.

                    To more than inland peace
Left by the west wind sweeping overhead
From a tumultuous ocean, trees and towers
In that sequestered valley may be seen,
Both silent and both motionless alike;
Such the deep shelter that is there, and such
The safeguard for repose and quietness.
   Our steeds remounted and the summons given,
With whip and spur we through the chauntry flew
In uncouth race, and left the cross-legged knight,
And the stone-abbot, and that single wren
Which one day sang so sweetly in the nave
Of the old church, that—though from recent showers
The earth was comfortless, and touched by faint
Internal breezes, sobbings of the place
And respirations, from the roofless walls
The shuddering ivy dripped large drops—yet still
So sweetly 'mid the gloom the invisible bird
Sang to herself, that there I could have made
My dwelling-place, and lived for ever there
To hear such music. Through the walls we flew
And down the valley, and, a circuit made
In wantonness of heart, through rough and smooth
We scampered homewards.